Cheaters Always Prosper

Cheaters Always Prosper

50 Ways to Beat the System Without Getting Caught

James Brazil

A Citadel Press Book
Published by Carol Publishing Group

A Citadel Press Book
Published by Carol Publishing Group
Citadel Press is a registered trademark of Carol Communications, Inc.

Editorial, sales and distribution, rights and permissions inquiries should be addressed to Carol Publishing Group, 120 Enterprise Avenue, Secaucus, N.J. 07094

In Canada: Canadian Manda Group, One Atlantic Avenue, Suite 105, Toronto, Ontario, M6K 3E7

Carol Publishing Group books may be purchased in bulk at special discounts for sales promotion, fund-raising, or educational purposes. Special editions can be created to specifications. For details, contact Special Sales Department, 120 Enterprise Avenue, Secaucus, N.J. 07094.

Manufactured in the United States of America
10 9 8 7 6 5 4 3 2 1

Library of Congress Cataloging-in-Publication Data
Brazil, James.
    Cheaters always prosper : 50 ways to beat the system without being caught / James Brazil.
        p.   cm.
    "A Citadel Press book."
    ISBN 0-8065-1809-X
    1. Crime—Miscellanea.   2. Consumer education—Miscellanea.
3. Saving and thrift—Miscellanea.   I. Title.
HV6030.B75 1996
364.1—dc20   96-9770
                                                              CIP

Contents

Contents

Introduction

This book was written with the encouragement of some of my friends who have always turned to me when they needed advice on getting out of something, into something, making easy money, and other such miracles. I wrote this book for all the people out there who play by the rules and wonder why other people get ahead. In short, rules were made to be broken. One needs to stand back and look at the system once in a while and see how it really works. That is, look at the under-the-table arrangements, the payoffs, the you-scratch-my-back-and-I'll-scratch-yours deals and the blatant ripoffs that are part and parcel of our society.

I figured out how the world works when I was fifteen and working at a very prestigious country club in California. I got the job because I was being a nice guy to the new kid at my high school. His name was Aaron, and his locker was next to mine. Having been to ten or so schools myself by that time, I knew the awkward and scared feelings of being the new kid, so I introduced myself to him. We ate lunch together and hung out that weekend. It turned out that his father had just moved their family to my area because he had been hired as the new tennis pro at a select membership country club about ten minutes away from where I lived. My parents were breathing down my neck to get a job because I was old enough to start learning the value of money... get a job... blah, blah, blah, and something about money and trees.

I was pissed and complaining to Aaron about what a drag it was, and he suggested that I get a job as a caddie at the country club where his father worked. Aaron had just started working there, and I was impressed with the tips he was making and the people he was meeting. If the names of the people he caddied for were not in the opening credits of every major movie I saw, they were on the front page of the *Los Angeles Times* business section on a daily basis. The job sounded a lot more appealing than Food Preparation Technician (McDonald's employee) or Petroleum Transfer Engineer (Chevron full-serve boy), positions that other kids had taken. I decided to apply.

Hurdle No. 1: I had to be eighteen to work there. Solution: Aaron told me to lie about my age. I did. It worked.

Hurdle No. 2: They wanted documentation of my age (for insurance purposes, of course). Aaron had lied, too, but had not needed documentation; apparently it would have been bad form to ask the head tennis pro's son for proof of his age. I did have the problem. Solution: My mother's secretary took pity on me. She falsified a few documents with some white-out, a typewriter, and a copy machine that gave the country club a paper trail. When I gave the paperwork to the caddie master, he smiled a knowing smile when he saw the Xeroxed documents—and handed me the caddie test.

Hurdle No. 3: The caddie test. I failed miserably. The questions about caddie etiquette and rules were simple; they were common-sense answers. The problem was that more than half of the test comprised maps of each hole on the course, and I had to fill in yardages from all the natural landmarks on a hole in relation to the putting green. For example, "this tree is 217 yards from the edge of the putting green, and this rock formation is..." I told Aaron that I had failed. He told me I was stupid; no one passed the test without cheating. Solution: I cheated on my makeup test—purposely leaving one wrong answer—and I passed and prospered.

Hurdle No. 4: I got the job, but I didn't even know how to play golf. Solution: I bulled my way through the first few rounds and learned quickly. (The game is so simple that I had to laugh at the people who played it.)

So there I was, at age fifteen, caddying for movie stars, producers, captains of industry—and making $75 to $100 per round. I was meeting incredible people, spending my days on a world-class golf course, and getting paid four or five times as much as friends who had routine jobs. What did I do? I got greedy. I wanted more money, and it was there.

There were some members of the club who were "new money" in every sense of the term. The caddies loved them because they were the people who thought it was classy to tip for anything and everything. Carry their bag from their car to a golf cart (forty or so yards), and you'd have ten dollars for lunch. These people were also major tippers for a round of golf. A lot of them were professional sports players (or owned a team) and felt that the size of the tip was a measure of their masculinity. These golfers were a real prize for a caddie; $200 to $500 per round was standard. These were the rounds every caddie wanted but only a few of us got.

Now, I understood that there was a hierarchy involved and I was at the end of the line, but I was not satisfied with this arrangement. I worked my ass off for every round and players loved me, so I talked to the caddie master about getting the better-paying rounds. I was told that certain caddies had been around much longer and had more experience and, in a roundabout way, that I should "shove it." I continued to work diligently for a measly $75 to $100 per round as I watched certain caddies making, what I computed to be, over $50,000 a year, in cash. After a while

I finally got the chip off my shoulder and decided to become close to some of them and learn from their infinite caddying wisdom. I learned to kiss a little more tush, which raised my earnings slightly but I still was not getting the best rounds.

One day one of the more experienced caddies took me aside and explained to me how to get the good rounds. In doing so, he also taught me how the world works. He was leaving the club to follow his dream of becoming a professional golfer, and he recognized my work ethic and my frustration. The trick was simple; I had to give the caddie master 10 percent of my tips under the table, and he would make sure I was getting the best-paying rounds. I started paying off the caddie master, and I became the richest fifteen-year-old around. The $200 to $500 rounds were now mine too, along with front-row tickets to more major sporting events than I could ever attend.

Caddying for people at this club taught me more about the road to success than any class or book possibly could. I learned that an education is by no means a prerequisite for success. I witnessed multimillion-dollar deals being cut over golf games, and the little extras thrown in to the deals that could not be described as anything other than payoffs. In short, I received the best education on how the world really operates by seeing the inner workings that outsiders are not supposed to see. I put this book together to reveal some of the inner workings that make up our capitalist society to readers who are sick of playing by the rules but still have not figured out how to break them and get away with it. I have tried most of what appears on the following pages and gotten away with almost everything.

Cheaters Always Prosper

1

Screwing the Supermarket

Here's how to eat very well for very little money: Go to the butcher section of the local supermarket and order two pounds of jumbo shrimp at $14.99 per pound and two pounds of beef by-products (for the dog, of course) at 79¢ per pound. Both of the packages are wrapped in white butcher paper with price stickers on them. Switch the labels and ditch the beef by-products behind some frozen TV dinners. When you pay for your shrimp, you are charged for the beef by-products on the price sticker. This is a great method for buying choice cuts of meat and other expensive butcher items. Note: Watch out for cameras in the ceiling of the supermarket, as well as employees

moving around through the store. If you are caught peeling the labels off, just say you were checking the freshness of the meat and you accidentally put the labels back on the wrong package.

You can also try the following: A girl-friend baked a birthday cake for a surprise party thrown for me and it turned out perfectly. It was honestly delicious and everyone loved it, but for some reason the baker was totally dissatisfied with the way the cake turned out. Perhaps it was in my honor that she did what she did. Whatever the reason, I was impressed with her actions. She took the empty packages—boxes, icing, etc.—back to the store with her receipt. The key thing that she brought back to the store, however, was the carton of milk used to make the cake. Although the milk was fresh, she poured a little lime juice into it, which gave it a rotten odor and curdled it. She took all of the cake ingredients to a store manager, had him smell the milk and demanded a refund. She told him that everyone who had eaten the cake suffered food poisoning and that the party had been ruined. The manager was apologetic and he not only refunded all the cake mix ingredients, but he gave her a $150 gift certificate for purchasing other groceries. This scam can be worked with many different kinds of food in the market.

2

Free Meals in Expensive Restaurants

When traveling, I go to the most expensive restaurants available. I always run up large tabs with good wine, appetizers, entrees, and then dessert. Dessert is the surprise because I bring a small bag of shards of broken glass to the table. I put a shard of glass in the dessert and then call the waiter over about it. I tell him that I cut my mouth on the glass and to check the kitchen to be sure that no other food has broken glass in it because some customers would sue over something like this. Usually the manager or owner is at my table within thirty seconds kissing my butt and refusing to let me pay for the meal. I accept.

Sometimes however, I run into people who suspect me of planting the glass, and they are much more difficult to deal with. One time, the manager wouldn't buy my story. I had the dessert removed from the tab but had to pay $120 for the rest of the meal. Since then, I have added a climax to the routine.

Most costume shops sell capsules of fake blood. The capsules are filled with syrupy sugar-water that looks like blood. During dessert, I crush a couple of them in my teeth, and let a little bit dribble down my cheek. Then I spit some of the fake blood on my napkin and make sure it is all over my teeth when I call the waiter over to show him the shard of glass. This works every time but I now have to make sure that no one calls an ambulance. I always leave a good tip for the waiter or waitress.

If you still want to eat for free or at a discount and not have to make a scene, never underestimate the power of complaining. In the restaurant business the customer is always right, and this can be exploited. Pick any corporate chain of restaurants. Call the corporate office to complain about bad service, food, environment, etc. Tell the customer service department that you were treated rudely or ignored or that you received an unsatisfactory meal, and you can be sure that they will offer you another meal, gratis, to keep you as a satisfied customer. Fast-food restaurants will usually give you restaurant coupons, and

more upscale restaurants, more likely a gift certificate for lunch or dinner for two. Just tell them that you have been a loyal customer, and request the complimentary meal if they do not offer it.

The following are some workable complaints: Bad service; rude waiter; dirty, hung-over-looking waiter; flat drinks; cold food; stale bread; dirty dishes; dirty environment (restaurant and restrooms); something foreign in the food; etc. Be creative!

There is one more way to get a free meal. I have been to restaurants that have picked up my check because I sat in chewing gum in a booth or chair. I wear pants that I do not care about or jeans from which gum can be removed, and I plant some chewed gum on my seat. Then I complain that the pants were very expensive and that they have been ruined. The manager will usually waive the tab for this, too.

All You Can Eat... for a Week

There's another restaurant trick which is applicable to the all-you-can-eat buffet setup. I learned the following from older and wiser friends in college: bring Tupperware in a bag when you go out to a meal at an all-you-can-eat establishment. Fill the containers with food from your plate and tray. A woman can also line a tote-bag or purse with aluminum foil and just empty her plate into the bag.

It is best to choose an out of the way table so other diners aren't staring at you. I also recommend bringing bags or anything else that does not look conspicuous on the table but will conceal your packaging procedures. You can make enough trips to have food for days. This is also a very practical way to save time on cooking since you can microwave the leftovers. Note: Try to pick foods that will last in your refrigerator. Many types of food are only good when they have been freshly prepared.

3

Free Food and Booze in Hotels

Many large hotels contain restaurants and bars. When I travel, I also eat and drink in hotels because I can put the bill on someone else's tab. I wait until I see someone leaving his hotel room and note the room number. After I make sure he is not checking out, I can tell waitresses to charge food and drinks to "my room" (which is actually the room of the other person).

In most cases you will have to sign for whatever you order. When you sign for it, look on the tab and you will usually find the name of the person footing the bill next to the room number. I recommend signing the name in a scrawl. If the name of the person to whose room you are charging your bill is not on the tab when you have to sign it, just write in completely illegible pigeon-scratch, and they won't know the difference. (See a doctor's signature on a prescription for a good example of a completely illegible signature.)

If you do get the name of the person from the tab, make a note of it. Then, if you really have chutzpah, you can request the hotel limo driver to take you to nightclubs, theaters, and so on. It is best to call the front desk and request the limo so you do not have to see the clerks in person, who might recognize you. The request should be as follows: "Hello, this is John Doe in Room 314. I'm having a drink in the lounge, and I was wondering if I could get the hotel limo to drop me off at _____?" Sometimes you will find that the limo has already been reserved, but they will usually squeeze you in for a quick trip if you turn on the charm. If all goes well, they tell you the limo will be waiting in front of the hotel for you at the time you requested. Don't worry about any charges to the room of the person you are impersonating, because he will not have to pay the bill if he refutes the charges. By that time you had better be long gone.

Free Stay at Hotels (Without the Room)

Another great aspect of large hotels is that you can stay at them without taking a room. When I was in college, my friends and I traveled all over the country in a convertible during the summer. We would sleep under the stars every night and freshen up in comfortable hotels in the mornings. The staff at large hotels never know who is a guest and who is not, so when we walked into a hotel and acted like actual guests, we were treated like them.

Usually the upscale hotels have a swimming pool, hot tub, tennis court, and men's and women's bathrooms by the pool so that people can shower and dry off before going back inside. We would use these bathrooms to get cleaned up after a morning swim or tennis game. In some resort areas, like Palm Springs, we would spend an entire day lounging around the pool where live bands played reggae music. We were playing volleyball, meeting new people, and charging everything to other people's rooms. We traveled through North America in grand style and hardly paid for anything. The key to pulling it off was acting like we were staying in the hotel. If we hopped a fence to get into the pool security would nail us. On the other hand, when we walked through the lobby with bags we looked like guests. This is a good example of how to get away with something by being completely obvious about it.

Free Towels, Toiletries, and Tea

Often the bathrooms in five-star hotels will have all the necessary toiletries laid out for your use. This is always a great way to stock up on towels for your own living quarters. I have a collection of white towels that furnish every bathroom in my house. All the extras are great for dishrags and washing and waxing cars.

Mornings in hotels are also good for complimentary continental breakfasts, which are commonly laid out buffet-style for the guests. If I bring reuseable containers, I can usually steal enough food for lunch, too. Hotels are also a great place to pick up a nice set of silverware instead of buying it. A buffet setup often leaves all of the spoons, knives, and forks out for the guests to take for themselves. Dishes are a little harder to steal, and hotel dishes usually look like hotel dishes, but if you want them... well, there's no accounting for taste.

4

Borrowing Brand-New Cars

One morning I woke up knowing I had to drive down the coast to have lunch with a friend and pick up some paperwork. It was such a beautiful day that I absolutely had to drive a convertible. I refuse to pay money to rent a cheesy convertible, so I set my mind to borrowing a fancy one. I went to the Ford dealership and told a salesman that a relative had just left me some money and I wanted to treat myself to a convertible. I test drove a fully-loaded Mustang GT convertible and I told the dealer everything he wanted to hear such as "I love it, I want it, It's a great

price." (It was overpriced by five thousand dollars.) I could almost see the commission dollar signs spinning in his eye sockets. He asked me what he could do to make me drive home in the Mustang that day. My response was that I wanted to drive it around for the day and get a better feel for the car. Five minutes later, they had filled the tank and sent my on my merry way. When I returned it, I told the dealer that I had promised to look at my mother's friend's Mustang, which she had just bought and did not like. I said she was offering it to me for a great price, but that I hated the color, so I would be back in the morning to buy the one I borrowed. I never called him back.

Two days later I had to drive down the coast again and had the same dilemma: beautiful day and no convertible. This time I went to the BMW dealership and gave the dealer the same line. He was a tougher egg to crack because he wanted proof that I had the money in the form of bank statements. This was a big hurdle. I had to have that convertible BMW, though, so I went to my bank. I deposited a $75 check into my account and entered $75,000 at the cash machine where I made my deposit. It gave me a transaction receipt that said my balance was over $75,000. I then took out some money and used the receipt to show the dealer. I also went inside the bank and told the teller I was in a rush and I had made a mistake in my deposit. She was very nice and fixed it for me immediately. I still had the receipt. I showed it to the dealer, and I was out the door with a convertible BMW for the day.

5

New Paint Job and New Windshield for Free

My car's windshield had a crack in it, and I got a ticket before I had a chance to have it fixed. I did not want to pay for the new windshield or the ticket. While I was driving one day, I made a note of some government workers repairing the road near my home. They were patching and repaving parts of the highway, and there were pebbles and gravel all over the road. I went to a car dealership and got an estimate for a new windshield (and for a new paint job for the front of my car while I was at it). The estimate was about $2,400, and I sent a copy of it with a copy of my cracked-windshield ticket to the state highway department. In my letter to them, I asked them to pay for the windshield, the paint, and the ticket. I figured that they would refute the claim or try to pay for only a percentage of the bill. Instead, they sent me a check for the entire amount I had asked for. I paid my ticket, replaced my windshield, and pocketed the remaining $2000. Of course, the tiny nicks on the front of my car were pre-existing and hardly noticeable, so I just spent the paint job money that the state highway department gave me on a vacation.

A similar way to get a windshield replaced, and even make money on the side, works as follows: I keep an eye out when I am driving (especially on highways) for trucks carrying gravel. I write down the name, city, and phone number of the trucking company and send it a bill like the one I sent to the state highway department. I sent several trucking companies the same bill and got money from all of them. I also sent the bill to a few city government offices saying that gardeners mowing the lawns in the center dividers of major streets accidentally shot a rock through the lawn mower and cracked my windshield. They also sent me money. The most important part of all these claims is that you must provide the date, time, and place of the incident, because most companies and government agencies will check to see if their workers were where you say they were at the time your claim notes.

6

Speeding Tickets and Related Offenses

I was pulled over for speeding and the officer was a real tough egg. Admittedly, I was going over eighty miles per hour, but I feel that I can drive safely at such speeds. The officer did not, and he gave me a fat ticket. If this ticket went on my record, I would have had my license suspended because of some other ridiculous tickets that I had received previously. I went to court and pleaded "not guilty," and was given a court date to plead my case against the officer. In traffic court, if the officer does not show up for the case hearing, the ticket and charges are dropped.

The officers are paid to go to court so they generally go, but sometimes people get lucky and they do not show up. I had to make sure that the officer did not show up so I drafted the following letter:

Dear Officer _____

My name is Gary Wolfe and I have been named the executor of the will of John McFarlin who passed away on February 11, 1993. He left you five thousand dollars for saving his life in California. I cannot be sure it was you. However, Mr. McFarlin did have a very close friend in Montclair, California, whom he visited regularly. I will be in the Los Angeles area on February 26th through the 28th taking care of other business regarding Mr. McFarlin's estate. Please join me for breakfast at 9:00 A.M. at the Sidewalk Cafe restaurant in the Westin Bonnaventure Hotel in downtown Los Angeles. I will have your check and a picture of Mr. Randall so you can identify him and hopefully tell me something which might validate your claim. Due to the fact that the will was handwritten, it does not hold much legal weight. In short, all unclaimed assets will be turned over to the state so it would be in your best interest to show up. I look forward to meeting you.

Sincerely,
Gary Wolfe

The meeting date in this letter happened to coincide with my court date. I left no return address, phone number, or even fingerprints on the letter. I addressed it to the California Highway Patrol, Attn. Officer _____. Then I sent the letter in an envelope to my friend in New Hampshire who dropped it in the mail there so it sported a New Hampshire postmark.

When the court day came around the officer did not show up, and the judge said it was my lucky day. I don't know how much luck had to do with it but I'm still driving.

7

Protecting Your Driving Record

At one point my driver's license was suspended, so I went to Vancouver, Canada, and got a Canadian license using a friend's address. I used it to drive during the time my license was suspended in California, and any speeding tickets I got were sent to the address in Vancouver. The great advantage of this was the fact that I could get an unlimited number of tickets in California, and nothing would go on my record in the United States, because the departments of motor vehicles in the United States and Canada do not communicate with each other. I have some

Canadian friends who get tickets in the United States and don't even pay them. Unfortunately, getting a driver's license from a state other than your own won't work in this scenario because the departments of motor vehicles from all the states communicate with each other to make sure people's driving records are kept in focus wherever they go in the United States. Canadian licenses are easy to get; this applies to Mexican licenses as well.

8

New Tires for Free

I needed new tires for my car, and I was on the way to buy them until a friend told me how to get them for free. I rented a car that had the same size tires as the ones on my car. Then a friend helped me swap the tires between the rental car and my car. Instead of paying $400 for a new set of tires, I ended up paying $35 for a car rental. I also switched the air filters since they were compatible.

When I returned the car minus a few components, the rental company employees didn't notice. Rental cars are great sources of all sorts of miscellaneous parts that can be used on other cars.

Note: It is best to swap tires with a rental car before your own tires are actually balding. Bald tires are obvious, and you run the risk of an inspector noticing the switch. On the other hand, if your tires are well worn but not balding, it will look like normal wear and tear on the rental vehicle.

9

Avoiding Mileage Charges on Rental Cars and Vans

Another idea for use with rental cars is to turn off the odometer, which keeps the mileage charges down. This can be done very simply by pulling the fuse for the dashboard. The speedometer and the lighting in the dash won't work, but the radio will not be affected, so you can travel with music and the headlights will still function. The owner's manual for the car will show you where the fuse box is located. In most manuals there is a diagram that will point out which fuse controls the dashboard. They are easy to remove and replace.

This method can also be used to keep the recorded mileage down on your own car. For purposes of convenience, I recommend installing a switch on the dashboard fuse that can be turned on and off from the driver's seat. This enables the driver to turn it off so that miles do not continue to register. Note: It is important to keep a mental note of your actual mileage so that you do not miss oil changes and other important maintenance services.

10

Flying First Class for Coach Fare

When traveling, I buy coach-class plane tickets but fly first class. This is easy to do, because when the flight attendants announce the boarding of the plane, I wait until the final boarding call. At this time, almost all of the people on the flight are in their seats. When I board the plane, I sit in any open seat that I see in first class. Because I am one of the last people to board, it is very unlikely that I am in someone else's seat since everyone else is already seated. Because I am in first class, the flight attendants do not want to run the risk of offending me by asking me if I have a first-class ticket, so I usually do not have any problems once the seat belt is fastened. If they do catch me, I tell them that I booked a first-class seat but the ticket counter made a mistake and gave me coach. Then I offer to pay extra for the seat. In most cases this is fine with the flight attendants. Later, when the airline calls to ask me to pay the difference, I tell the airline that I refuse to pay for first class when I was treated so rudely. I describe how I was asked to leave the first-class section which I requested when buying the ticket. It is especially easy to find a seat in first class on large planes, such as 747s. The hassles usually come on smaller planes where the flight attendants know exactly who should be in each seat. In all cases I recommend being polite and cordial to the flight attendants, even if you are being stubborn. Otherwise they will probably spit in your food.

11

New Clothes at the Airlines' Expense

Sometimes when flying, I check a carry-on sized bag in at the baggage desk with my other bags so that I have a claim tag on each bag. The clerk at the desk will then staple one claim-tag number stub to my ticket for each bag that I check in. When I go to claim my baggage at my destination I pick up all my luggage, but I rip the tag off of the carry-on. Of course, I have to be inconspicuous about removing the tag, but this is not difficult in the usual airport crowds.

I then go to the airline desk at the airport and claim that

one of my bags did not arrive. I show them my matching claim-tag number stubs for all my baggage that I did get, and I show them my claim-tag number stub for the missing bag. If they ask about my carry-on bag, I tell them that I brought it onboard with me and did not check it. When they search their records, they find that I am indeed missing one bag and that it was indeed checked in. I describe an expensive garment bag loaded with clothes, cameras, etc. Then I tell the people at the airline desk that I am traveling on business and that the missing bag had all of my business suits in it, and I need one for a meeting that day.

Airline policy is usually to replace any lost articles. They explain this to me, and I go shopping and spend a lot of money on new clothes. Then I send the airline the bill. The always reimburse me for my clothes, and sometimes I am credited with free plane tickets as compensation for my trouble.

12

Free Airline Tickets and Their Cash Value

I obtained my first Porsche with the following swindle: I buy plane tickets on the busiest flights leaving my city. These flights are usually overbooked by the airlines. (I found out through a flight attendant friend which flights were consistently overbooked. Travel agents have this information too.) I buy the tickets for full price through the airline ticket counter, using a credit card so that they are fully refundable. When airlines have overbooked flights, they ask the passengers if anyone will be willing to take a later flight. I always offer to be bumped. Many airlines have a policy of offering a free round-trip plane ticket to any destination in the continental United States to anyone who gets bumped. I get this free ticket as compensation, and then I return my ticket at the ticket counter saying that I want to take the flight a few days later. They credit my card with the price of the ticket, and I leave with a free ride to anywhere in the continental United States. If the flight that I expected to get bumped from is not over-booked I do the same thing; I return the ticket at the ticket counter saying that I changed my mind and I do not want to fly that day (I do not get stuck paying for a ticket). Then I buy a ticket for another flight that is likely to be overbooked and try again. The great thing about getting a free plane ticket is that it can actually be sold to a travel agency or a private party. These free round-trip tickets go for anywhere from four hundred dollars to six hundred dollars. I sold a batch of such tickets to a travel agency and bought a car with the money. I also used some for travel around the country.

13

Making Money Returning Purchases

This swindle can be applied in various ways, but I will offer a specific example: You buy five small-size Ralph Lauren Polo shirts at one store where they sell for $32 each. At another more upscale department store, you return them, saying that they were a gift from a relative who did not know your size. You say you do not want them, and the department store will send you a check reimbursing you for the shirts at the retail price—$55 per shirt. In short, you make a $23 profit on each shirt by buying them where they are cheap and returning them where they are expensive. Note: Do not go into the store looking like a bum when you do this. If you look respectable, you are less likely to be suspected of fraud. Again, be courteous when you are dealing with the sales representatives, and you will get less of a hassle.

14

Getting Paid to Shop

After Christmas, when stores are busy with returns, you can go shopping and take the tags off of clothes (inconspicuously) and return them for cash. This can actually be done any time of year, but you are less likely to be noticed in the after-Christmas crowds. You simply take the tags off of the items you pick, throw them away, and go to the counter and say they were gifts and you want to return them. You can also exchange them for other clothes in the store. When they ask for the receipt, just tell them it was lost in the holiday shuffle. They will probably hassle you, but be persistent and you will get a refund. Sometimes they will ask you if you would like them to send you a check or just give you a credit. This is always a great way to shop without paying for anything.

15

New Apparel Every Week

Because it is important to look good in business, I always wear very nice new clothes. This would be an expensive habit, but I never pay for them. Instead, I go shopping and buy one week's worth of expensive clothes on a credit card. I wear them all week, being careful not to damage them, and then I return them. I tell the people where I return the clothes that they were a gift for a friend who was leaving the country and that I did not get the clothes to my friend before he left. I have the entire bill recredited to my card, and then I go shopping in another store and do the same thing.

16

Free Money From Credit Cards

For those people who need money but cannot get a loan, credit cards are the answer. Usually a person has only a limited number of credit cards. If, for example, I do not have much credit history, and I already have five well-used credit cards, I am likely to be turned down when I apply for a sixth card. The credit card companies check my credit with my Social Security number, which is on my application. When they check this they see that I already have five credit cards and they reject me. If, however, I have no credit cards and I apply for twenty or thirty credit cards all at the same time (mail them on the same day), they will all be approved because they all check my credit at the same time and see that I have no cards. Then, when I receive my credit cards I can get cash advances on half of them and not use the other half. When I get my bills, I pay the first half of them off with the other half and so on and so on.

For example, I get twenty credit cards. I take $1,000 in cash advances from each of the first ten credit cards. When I get billed for these cards I take cash advances of $1,000 from each of the other ten credit cards to pay the bills for the first ten credit cards. Every month I pay off one half of the credit cards with the other half. By doing this, I avoid paying any interest on my credit cards because the first thirty days are interest-free on charges made on all major credit cards. The only charges I incur are the relatively small charges for taking cash advances on the cards. In most cases these charges are less than the interest rates on a bank loan. This is a great way to give yourself some spending money without having to repay. A person could theoretically run this scheme forever.

17

Reward Money for Lost Pets

A college acquaintance was told by his parents to earn his own spending money but he was allergic to working. One day he found a wandering dog and took it home with him. A few days later, he saw reward signs around his neighborhood. He returned the lost dog to the grateful owner, who rewarded him with $100. He then began picking up animals in upscale neighborhoods and keeping them at his home until he saw reward signs. Then he would return the animals and collect the rewards. He did quite well doing this, and when he did not see reward

signs, he would call the numbers on the pets' ID tags (if they had one) and tell the people that he had just found the pet. Usually he would get a reward for this, too. It was easy money for him, and it only cost him a minimal amount to feed the pets.

18

Vending Machines

I never pay for food from vending machines because I always get my money back after I get the food. Here's how: Take a strip of clear heavy-duty packing tape (used at the post office) and tape a strip that is one and a half dollar-bill lengths long to the short edge of a dollar bill. Place an equal length of tape to the other side so that the sticky sides of the tape are stuck together. The tape should overlap the edge of the dollar bill by approximately one-eighth of an inch so that it barely covers any of the face on the bill. Keep this bill in your wallet or purse and use it at vending machines any time. Here's how it works: You insert the bill into the bill receiver and let it slide all the

way into the machine where it stops to be read. Hold on tightly to the tape that is still sticking out of the receiver. Make your selection, and pull the taped bill out. You will get whatever you selected and change on top of getting your bill back.

Free Money From Vending Machines

Some older-model vending machines have bill receivers that have an adverse reaction to salt water. By pouring salt water in the bill-receiver slot, a person can make the bill reader short-circuit and cause the vending machine to spit out all of its change. It does not have to be ocean water; any salt and water solution will work. Unfortunately, only older models react this way. The newer models are immune to this particular trick.

19

Free Laundry

I learned this trick in the dormitories, but it also has other applications. For this example, we will use a Laundromat. The slots on many pay washing machines and dryers take coins in an upright position in a series of parallel horizontal slots. I borrow an old pair of panty hose and place a layer of it over the quarter slots. Then I put the quarters into the slots with the thin layer of panty hose under them. I fold the top layer of panty hose over the top of the quarters and push the coin tray into the vending machines. The quarters go into the machine in the slots, but the thin layer of panty hose prevents them from falling into the coin box inside the machine. Instead, the quarters return, and the machine is still activated.

20

Bad Checks

Need a new stereo, TV, dining room set, etc.? If you find or get hold of somebody else's checkbook you can buy almost any used item in the classified section of a newspaper or in magazines. This is because most people in residences generally do not ask for identification. You also do not have to worry about being recorded by a hidden camera. You can write bad checks for just about anything. It is not a good idea to do this in the area where you live, however, because of the risk of running into someone you've scammed.

21

Free Compact Disks and Tapes

In magazines, you can often find order forms for mail-order record clubs. These clubs attract members by offering several tapes or CDs for free when you join up. They make their money by getting members to commit to buying more CDs at inflated prices.

I have hundreds of CDs because I order these free introductory packages under false names. They send me several CDs up front, and then bill the false name. The bills eventually turn into threats to ruin the credit of that nonexistent person; the record companies turn over overdue bills to a collection agency. Of course, I never pay, and just order more CDs under new names. Sometimes they put a freeze on any CDs coming to my address, but I just rent a P.O. box, and then another, and another...

This works well with magazine subscriptions and anything else you can order through the mail. I just check the "bill me" box on the order form and use a false name.

22

Discounts on New Merchandise

Whenever I want to buy something new, I apply for a job at a place that retails whatever it is that I want to buy. As soon as I get the job, I buy whatever it is that I want with my employee discount, and then quit. Employee discounts commonly pass the items along to the employees at cost. This means that the retailer sells the item to the employee for the same price that the company buys it from the manufacturer. With electronics, the discount is usually one third to one half off the retail price; with new automobiles, the discount is commonly between one-quarter and one-half off the retail price. With furniture, the discounts are often more than fifty percent off the retail price.

If I cannot get a job where I want to an employee discount, or if I do not want the hassle, I approach an employee and cut a deal. I usually offer them fifty to one hundred dollars to buy something for me using my money. In this case you have to be careful, however, because you leave yourself wide open to be ripped off, and you do not have much recourse. Make sure you trust someone before cutting a deal like this.

23

Résumés

Everybody knows that people embellish résumés a little bit. I embellish a lot and it never seems to catch up with me. In today's job market you do not want to be qualified; you want to be overqualified. A résumé says just as much about a person—if not more—than an actual interview. Without a stand-out résumé you may not even get an interview.

I once saw a comedian who gave me my theory on résumé writing. He said his mother could never accept him because he did not go to college. She said to him, "Just go to college so you can tell people you have a degree." His response: "What? Like I can't say that now?"

It is a rather funny way of looking at things, but it is also quite true.

I went to college but I did not graduate. That does not look good on a résumé. I personally had a problem with taking classes that had no practical applications in my life so I took classes that I liked and received an education. I did not, however, get that piece of paper called a degree indicating I took all the classes I needed to graduate. I certainly do not state this on my résumé. I state that I graduated from the university I attended with a double major in Political Science and Business. I state that I graduated in four years, and that I was on the Dean's list for six of the eight semesters I was at school. I note that I was the president of many organizations including the Interfraternity Council and Saferides Program. I inflate the tiniest details into major events and I am able to lie very well when asked about anything on the résumé. In short, my entire résumé is created out of hot air. I know that employers in most fields are not going to ask me for proof of graduation or for transcripts so I say whatever puts me ahead of the other applicants. It still has not caught up with me and it does not look like it ever will.

24

Getting Several Salaried Jobs at Once

When I first started lying heavily on résumés, I obtained many of the jobs for which I applied. I decided to accept four salaried jobs at once. During my first month I reported a few family tragedies to all of the jobs and juggled all four of them, coming in to work only a few days each per month. I was even being interviewed for more jobs and accepting them. Upon accepting each job, I would come in to work, get set up, and meet everyone and establish good faith for the first couple of days. Then I would report these mythical family tragedies. I would

63

hardly show up at work after a while and drag out each job for as long as I could before they let me go. I usually got a month's pay and sometimes more. Of course this does not apply to hourly wage jobs, so you have to take only salaried positions. Another good rule of thumb is not to take any of these jobs in the area in which you live because you might run into company executives when you are ditching work.

25

Changing Prices

Many retail stores have stickers with bar codes on them stuck to their merchandise. The bar code is scanned over a laser at the checkout counter which reads the price. In many stores these stickers are removable. I switch the stickers with ones on lower-priced items, and the checkers usually don't notice. I did $30,000 worth of landscaping at my house for less than $4,000 by switching the stickers on plants, trees, and bushes in the nursery section of a major hardware store chain.

Some price stickers have the price of the item printed on the sticker, which is then manually entered into the cash register. I switch the price stickers and get away with

that, too. This usually works because cashiering is such a mindless job that cashiers are often disinterested. You can switch price stickers and bar codes and even price tags in many different kinds of stores, but be careful to avoid surveillance cameras.

26

Free Postage

When paying my bills, I put a one-cent postage stamp on the envelope instead of a thirty-two-cent stamp. I never put a return address on the envelopes, so the post office delivers it to the addressee with postage due. They will accept it and pay the thirty-one cents, because the company knows that the envelope contains a payment.

Another great way to send mail at no expense is to switch the addressee with the return address, and leave the postage off. Since there are no stamps on the letter, it will be "returned" to the address in the upper-left-hand corner of the envelope.

27

Taking an "Administrative Cut" From Charities

You can start any sort of charity and take a legal administrative cut. There are hundreds of ways of collecting money in the forms of fundraisers. Just organize a fundraiser, collect money for a charity, give the charity a small percentage of the money as a private donation, and keep the rest.

SAVE THE COCKROACH
FUND-RAISER

28

Switching Phone Companies for Cash Incentives

The war for customers between the phone companies has become so ridiculous that they will actually pay customers cash to switch from one company to another. I call up one of the big three companies each month and ask what they will offer if I switch to their company and they do offer cash incentives to switch. I switch to a new company; they send me a check (usually up to fifty dollars), and then I do the same thing to a new phone company the next month. Sometimes the company I leave offers to send a check to stay with them.

29

Free Pizza and Other Delivered Food

I order food to be delivered to my neighbor's house, and while the delivery boy is ringing my neighbor's bell and trying to figure out where the delivery's supposed to go, I can take all the other food from the delivery car.

30

Replacing "Damaged" Goods

Just about every company has a department for handling customer service. If you send a product back to the manufacturer, you can bet that you will get a response and probably a new replacement. Here is an example:

I bought a couple of overpriced pairs of designer-label boxer shorts. They were very comfortable, so I wore them a lot. Of course, after a while they began wearing out. I took one pair and stretched it out as much as I could and sent it back to the manufacturer, along with a letter saying that I was not satisfied with the quality of their undergarments. I wrote that I had purchased seven pairs which were all in similar condition and that I wanted them all replaced. I complimented the company on its quality standards, and I said that I was otherwise a loyal customer who does not mind paying a premium for excellence. They sent me seven new pairs.

I do the same thing with just about every other product that wears out and everything is replaced, including shoes, electronics, sports equipment, etc.

31

Cut to the Front of the Line at Theme Parks

All my friends love to go with me to theme parks like Disneyland because I always fake a sprained ankle. Theme parks will offer a wheelchair to anyone who is disabled in any way. Park policy for wheelchair-bound visitors is to let them and all in their group cut to the front of the line. The best part of being in a wheelchair is that your friends push you around all day and your feet do not ache.

32

Charge Up a Credit Card and Report It Stolen

Here is a way to buy almost anything you want and not pay for it. Order a credit card and give it to one of your friends when it arrives. The friend can charge everything you want to buy in a very short space of time. Stores do not usually ask for an identification with a credit card but if your friend is caught he/she can be absolved because you can say that you gave permission to use it. Assuming your friend does not get caught however, you can call your credit card company when the statement arrives and report that the card was not received. Report that the card must have been stolen (after your friend finishes using it). Tell them you never had the card and that the charges were fraudulent. A credit card company does not charge you for unauthorized invoices so they take it as a loss and both you and the friend have everything that your friend charged, free of charge. You do have to be careful to lay low with the charged material as credit companies investigate these claims.

33

Have the Insurance Company Pay for an Uninsured Vehicle

My friend totaled his sports car and he did not have car insurance. He had it towed to his house without observation by the police. There was no report of the car being in an accident.

I had him borrow an identical automobile from another mutual friend, attach the license plates from the totaled car, and drive to an insurance broker. He purchased full collision coverage for the car which he had already totaled.

He gave the insurance agent all the paperwork from the wrecked car. She took a few Polaroid pictures of the pristine automobile. He paid the premium and returned the car to the other friend. One month later he called the insurance company and told them that he had been in an accident and had had his car towed to his home. He put in a collision claim and the company decided his car was totaled. The insurer gave him a check for a new car.

34

Other False Auto Insurance Claims

Some people scan the used car magazines for damaged cars that have a "clean title." This means that according to Department of Motor Vehicles' records the car is still in normal operating condition. Many cars that have been in accidents are given a "salvaged" label, which means that the damage from an accident was so severe that it is cheaper for the insurance company to replace the car than pay to have it fixed. This "salvaged" title goes on the Department of Motor Vehicles' records. If however, a car has been in an accident, and there is no documentation of the accident at the Department of Motor Vehicles, the car has a "clean title." This means that you can usually buy the damaged vehicle at a highly discounted price and have it insured, using a car that is exactly the same model (to show the insurance company when you purchase insurance). Again you can submit a bogus claim using your damaged car after you have it insured as an automobile in sound working order. They will pay to have your damaged car repaired or pay market value of the car if it had been in normal driving condition. Either way you will make money on the deal.

35

Homeowners' and Renters' Insurance

These types of insurance usually indemnify the holders against loss or damage. There are ways to make money from these policies.

For example, I sold all my electronics to friends and through the classifieds. Then I reported that I had been robbed one weekend while I was on vacation. My insurance company wrote me a check for a new TV, stereo, computer, mountain bike, and three portable phones. It is always a good idea to keep the receipts for these "stolen" items in your records so that you can give them to the insurance company, but you can usually get almost as much compensation without them. Of course, you can usually get compensation for just about anything that you report stolen from your house. The best part about these claims is that you get to pocket the cash from selling the equipment plus getting brand new replacements at the insurance company's expense.

36

Bogus Raffle Tickets

A couple that I know go to fairs, swap meets, and other similar events where they set up a table on the weekends to sell raffle tickets for their classic convertible. They display the convertible behind their booth and sell tickets for two to five dollars saying that proceeds go to charity. They never raffle off the car but they continue to collect for it and pocket the money from the ticket sales. They do, however, make contributions to the charity for which they are raising funds.

37

Free Admission to Movie Theaters and Concerts

When I go to the movies with friends, we only buy two tickets. The first two of our group go into the theater to be seated. Then one of them comes back outside with both of their tickets. He tells the ticket taker at the door that he left the car unlocked or something along those lines as an excuse to leave and come back. Then he gives the extra ticket to me and I enter the theater separately from my friend (who also re-enters the theater with his ticket). Then I take the two ticket stubs and repeat the same scenario and give one of the tickets to another in the group outside the theater.

This scam also has many other applications, including concerts where specified seats are not assigned. Two tickets can be recycled indefinitely if the people pulling the stunt are smooth.

38

Chain Letters

Never underestimate the stupidity of the public. Chain letters have been around for a long time and have made some people very rich. Others have at least made a moderate amount of money mailing them.

Chain letters are essentially a pyramid scheme. The following is a good example of a chain letter that works today. Note: You do not have to limit the amount of letters you send. The odds of making money greatly increase when you send chain letters to more people. Here is the letter:

My name is Dave Miller. In September 1991, my car was repossessed and bill collectors were hounding me like you wouldn't believe. I was laid off from work and my unemployment insurance had run out.

In October 1991, I received a letter telling me how to earn $50,000 anytime I wanted to. Of course I was skeptical, but because I was so desperate and virtually had nothing to lose, I gave it a try.

In January 1992, my family and I went on a ten-day cruise! The next month I bought a 1992 Cadillac with CASH! I am currently building a home in Florida and will never have to work again.

I have earned over $200,000 to date and I may have a million dollars within the next four to six months. This money program works perfectly every time and I have never failed to receive less than $50,000 with each mailing. This is a legitimate business opportunity; a perfectly legal money-making program. It does not require you to sell anything or to come in contact with people, and best of all, you only have to leave home to mail the letters.

If you believe that someday you will get that lucky break, simply follow the instructions below and your dream will come true!

Dave Miller, Palm Beach Florida

Follow these instructions exactly, and in twenty to sixty days you will receive over $50,000, guaranteed!

1. Immediately send $1.00 (cash only) to each of the five names listed below. Wrap up the dollar bill in a note

saying "Please add my name to your mailing list." This is a legitimate service for which you are paying $1.00.

2. Remove the name which is number one on the list and move the other four names up one position. (Number two will become number one, etc.) Then place your name in the number five position. This can be done easily by typing or printing the five names on a strip of paper and gluing or taping over the existing names on this sheet.

3. Photocopy or print two hundred or more copies of this letter which has your name now in the number five position.

4. Obtain a list of two hundred or more names of opportunity seekers from a mailing list company.

5. While waiting for your mailing list to arrive, place your copies in envelopes and stamp and seal them. Do not put your return address on the envelopes (this will pique the curiosity of the receiver!).

6. When your mailing list arrives, place one of the gummed address labels on each of your envelopes and drop them in the mail box.

Within sixty days you will receive your $50,000 in cash, guaranteed! Keep a copy of this letter for yourself so that you can use it again whenever you need funds. Go for it!

Note: As soon as you mail out these letters you are automatically in the mail order business, and people are sending you $1.00 to be placed on your mailing list. This is a service and is perfectly legal (refer to title 18, Sec. 1302 & 1341 of the U.S. postal and lottery laws).

Page two of the letter:

Now, here's the interesting part!
At a 7.5 percent response (which is very conservative):

1. When you send out 200 letters, 15 people will send you $15.00.
2. Those 15 will mail out 200 letters, of which 225 will send you $1.00, which equals $225.00.
3. Those 225 send out 200 letters, of which 3,375 will send you $1.00, equalling $3,375.00.
4. Those 3,375 send out 200 letters, so 50,625 will send you $1.00, totaling $50,625.00.

Sorry folks, that is as far as it goes, but you will receive:

$15.00
$225.00
$3,375.00
$50,625.00
$54,240.00

Letters written by participants in the program:

To whom it may concern:

About six months ago I received the enclosed letter. I ignored it. I received about five more of the same letters within the next few months. I threw them away too. I was tempted to follow through and make my quick thousands but I was convinced it was just a hoax and it could not possibly work. I was dead wrong! About three weeks later I decided to go ahead and give it a try. I didn't expect much because I figured if other people were as skeptical as I was, they wouldn't be too quick to respond. Two weeks went by and I didn't receive any money. Third week, still nothing. The fourth week rolled around and I couldn't believe what was happening! Within a few weeks, I had collected in excess of $32,000 in cash! For the first time in years I was debt-free. It didn't take me long to dry up that bundle so I am using this excellent money-making opportunity once again. Follow the instructions and get ready to enjoy!

C.R. Croft

Another letter:

I tried a similar program in which the cost was $5.00. In that one, the return was about 3 percent. The first time I sent letters with this approach, I got my first response in just one week! I sent out 500 letters instead of only 200 letters, so my responses were much higher and faster than my first attempt. I am trying again with 1000 letters this time to see if I surpass the $108,000.00 I collected last time. Good luck to all of you. It really has and will continue to work for you, just as it worked for me!

S. Ingram

Another letter:

I am a skeptical person by nature. I had received at least thirty-five different letters like this one in a six-month period. However, there was something about this particular letter that I liked. The initial investment was a great deal less than any of the other letters I had received before and I also liked the fact that all participants received money, not just the one in the top position. Anyway, I sent out 200 of these letters and hoped for the best. Every day I checked my mail hoping for a response. Nothing happened for eleven days. On day twelve I started to get a response. On that day I received $137.00 in the mail! I couldn't wait until the next day's mail. On day thirteen I received $909.00!! Over the next four and a half months I received $131,879 in the mail!!! Now that the letter I sent out seems to have run dry, I am going to try it again! I think I'll send out 1,000 letters this time. I hope I don't sound too greedy, but now that I have all this money, I want more.

J. O'Neil

Another note...

Been enjoying myself with all the bucks. This is the third time I have used this program. Funny, it keeps getting better each time around!

P. Thorp

39

Landscaping With Plants From Business Areas

Another way of avoiding paying for landscaping is to dig up plants from business areas. Many office complexes have attractive landscaping outside and in their parking lots. Often the plants, shrubs, and small trees are small enough that they can easily be dug up. I used to go to office parks at night and dig up greenery. Now, I hire workers to do it for me. One benefit of taking plants from office parks is that they are full-grown as opposed to the small, young plants available at a nursery. This is the cheapest way to landscape, but of course, the risks are obvious. I got the idea from a man who has a landscaping company. This is how he cuts costs.

40

How to Find Stolen Goods on the Black Market

We all know that there are black markets for anything that is smuggled or stolen. The question is, where does one go to purchase these black market items? The answer is: a city. Most big cities have an area known as "the shady side of town." It is the area that everyone is told to avoid if possible. This is also the area of any city to go to if you want to buy "hot" items such as electronics, jewelry, or car parts. Of course, stolen goods cannot be advertised in papers for obvious reasons, so these black markets are advertised through word-of-mouth.

I always look for seedy-looking characters on the street, or I try small businesses such as pawnshops and other one-owner stores. I never directly say that I am looking to buy stolen goods, but I imply it and try to evaluate the reactions of the individual I am asking. More often than not I come to a dead end, but it usually does not take me more than an hour or two to locate someone who can find what I want or knows someone who can. Note: Do not dress to "fit in" because you will look like an undercover cop. Be yourself when looking for black market goods, or the people you deal with will not trust or help you. Prices for stolen goods vary greatly but at least they are better than retail... and there is no tax! Do not forget that there is always room to bargain on the black market.

41

Free Refills on Perfumes and Cosmetics

A girl I know ran out of an expensive perfume and bought another bottle on her parents' credit card. Her parents told her to return it and not to waste their money on such items. I went with her to return it, and this is what we did: She put the near-empty bottle of perfume in the box from the new bottle. We went to the department store where she bought the perfume and we returned it. She told the saleswoman that the perfume gave her an allergic skin reaction. The saleslady recredited her credit card and she got to keep the new bottle.

42

All Green Lights

Most modern traffic stoplights are fitted with sensors that detect flashing lights. They are designed to clear the way for emergency vehicles (ambulances, fire trucks, etc.). When a stoplight senses flashing lights, it interrupts its normal changing pattern and sends a red light in all directions but the one from which the emergency vehicle is approaching. If you flash your brights several times at one of these signals, the flashing-light detector in the stoplight will react, giving you a green light. Of course, not all lights are equipped with this sensor, but the many that are make driving much faster.

43

Removing Locks

Here are a couple of methods of removing locks when you "lose your keys."

Many locks can be shattered by freezing them so cold that the metal becomes brittle. Freon and liquid nitrogen are both good for freezing locks. After a lock is frozen, it can usually be shattered by breaking it with a hammer.

Another method works well for U-locks used on bikes. Place a car jack in the middle of the U in the U-lock and jack it open. The metal will bend and then break.

44

How to Get a Handicapped Parking License

Do you hate to park miles from your destination? The solution is to have a disabled parking license. While you can steal one, the fine is hefty if you get caught with it. On the other hand, getting a legitimate handicapped license is not very difficult. All you need in most states is a letter from a medical doctor stating that you are handicapped in such a way that your mobility is impaired. Many handicaps are not openly visible. These are difficulties such as back problems (slipped disk or pinched nerve), or internal problems (like weak lungs or heart). Just go to your doctor and tell him or her that you have the symptoms for such a handicap. Ask for a letter stating that you are handicapped and have the doctor fill out any necessary forms. Then register with the Department of Motor Vehicles, and you will be sent a legitimate license plate for the handicapped.

45

The Concept of Payoffs in General

It is a fact that payoffs happen every day in our society. In cases where it's possible, one should attempt to cut an under-the-table deal. In most cases, the payoffs will be small, on-the-side arrangements. For example, a man from the telephone company came to install a phone line. I was already paying forty dollars to have the line connected at my home. To have an extra jack installed in my office, however, would cost an additional ninety dollars. When the man from the phone company came, I offered him twenty dollars in cash to run the line into my office.

Having all the necessary tools, he did it and left with twenty dollars in his pocket. The phone company was none the wiser, and it took him just an extra five minutes. This was just a minor payoff, but it is an example of how simple the concept of payoffs can be. Three out of four times you will find that people will make a deal with you if there is something in it for them.

46

Changing Your Fingerprints for Identification Purposes

If you ever need to have your fingerprints taken (for false identification or other records which you do not want traced to you), you can change your fingerprints. This is done by coating your fingers and thumbs with a thin layer of rubber cement. You then allow this to dry. Before the rubber cement has dried completely, press your fingers and thumbs firmly onto the palms of the opposite hand so that the skin pattern from the palm of your hand is imprinted on the rubber cement on your fingers/thumbs. Thus, your new fingerprints are actually backwards prints of the palms of your hands.

47

Degrees for Life Experience

If you have ever wished you had a degree, but couldn't be bothered to go to school to earn one, there is a solution. In the back of many magazines (usually business-oriented publications) there are advertisements for small correspondence colleges that give credits for "life experience." They usually offer a number of degree areas and if you cannot find one that suits you, they allow you to create your own. You actually mail in all of your work experience and degree requirements and they send you a degree. Of course, most of these mail-in colleges are not certified by the Department of Education, so they are not recognized as valid, but once again, who really checks up on this?

There is a way of getting around the problem of having a degree that is not recognized by the United States Department of Education: Some of the degrees are from correspondence universities outside the United States. If you obtain a degree from a university in another country, it still may not conform to U.S. degree requirements, but it is a degree on paper which might help you get a job. These colleges offer anything from a B.A. to an M.A.—and even a Ph.D! I am currently working on my dissertation for a Ph.D from a small college in England with a snotty name. Imagine... a doctorate in Bull...

48

Discounted Department Store Clothing

If you aren't daring enough to blatantly rip off department stores, here is a way for you to at least get a good discount: I learned this from a friend's mother who was always exquisitely dressed. She shops in the finest stores, finds what she wants and then, when she is in the changing room, she damages the clothing in some way that is hardly noticeable (e.g. unstitching or a discreet pen streak), yet leaves the garment undeniably flawed. Then she proceeds to purchase the garment, but she points out the defect to the salesperson before purchasing it. She asks for the garment's price to be reduced because of the flaw, and in almost every case she gets a very impressive discount with a manager's approval.

49

Warranties on Electronics

Take any piece of electronic equipment that is under warranty and make sure that a malfunction occurs (due to "product failure") just before the warranty ends so that the company has to replace the equipment. The best way of doing this with electronics is to plug them in and turn them on in a sauna-like environment, such as next to a hot shower, or a humidifier. The moisture seeps through into every crevice of the equipment and takes only a few hours to fry all the circuits inside. Then you give the electronic equipment a few days to dry out so that no traces of moisture are apparent. Finally you call the manufacturer of the electronic equipment and make your warranty claim. In most cases the manufacturer will replace the equipment with a new product, which has a new warranty.

I figured this out when a newer, more powerful model of my laptop computer came on the market, making the one I had obsolete. The beauty of this scam is that manufacturers will usually replace faulty equipment with their most current equivalent of that particular product. Thus, you maintain the most up-to-date electronics without paying for constant upgrades.

50

Catalog Merchandise for Keeps

The problem with using "borrowed" credit card numbers for catalog purchases is obvious; having anything delivered to a residence makes it pretty easy for the authorities to find you. There is a simple way around this. For catalog orders, you only need a credit card number, expiration date, and the cardholder's name to place an order, rather than the actual card. Credit card numbers are available to anyone who works in a retail store, restaurant, etc. Be careful not to take more than one or two numbers from one particular establishment because investigators will see this as a pattern and might investigate the people working there.

Once you have the numbers, you need to locate an uninhabited house/condo/office so that you have an address where merchandise can be delivered. The best places are out of the way of nosy neighbors, etc. Use discretion. Then, once you have located a delivery site, start ordering. In placing orders, you use the card number, its expiration date, and the name of the card holder as your own. Then of course, you give the address of the residence/office chosen. You may use the name on the card or have the package addressed to another name as a gift. Next, request overnight delivery on all of the merchandise so that you know exactly what day it will be delivered. Finally, set up a patio chair on the site chosen and pretend to be reading, or catching some sun or whatever else you can do at the site without having to go inside. Hang out for the day and sign for deliveries as they arrive. At the end of the day, throw everything in the car trunk and take off. The bank writes it off as a loss and collects insurance.

Do you have a favorite scam to take advantage of the system? If you do... send it to the attention of Citadel Press at 120 Enterprise Avenue, Secaucus, New Jersey 07094.

No compensation is involved but you might inspire a new version of this book.

More Interesting Books From Carol Publishing Group

Ask for the books listed below at your bookstore. Or to order direct from the publisher call 1-800-447-BOOK (MasterCard or Visa) or send a check or money order for the books purchased (plus $4.00 shipping and handling for the first book ordered and 75¢ for each additional book) to Carol Publishing Group, 120 Enterprise Avenue, Dept. 1809, Secaucus, NJ 07094.

Advanced Backstabbing and Mudslinging Techniques by George Hayduke, paperback $7.95 (#40560)

The Big Brother Game: Bugging, Wiretapping, Tailing, Optical and Electronic Surveillance, Surreptitious Entry by Scott French, oversized paperback $15.95 (#40241)

Disguise Techniques by Edmond A. MacInaugh, paperback $5.95 (#51098)

Find Them Fast, Find Them Now: Private Investigators Share Their Secrets for Finding Missing Persons by Frederick Charles Hoyer, Jr. and John McCann, oversized paperback $9.95 (#51080)

Getting Even by George Hayduke, oversized paperback $14.95 (#40314)

Getting Even 2 by George Hayduke, oversized paperback $12.95 (#40337)

How Con Games Work by M. Allen Henderson, paperback $9.95 (#51014)

How to Create a New Identity by Anonymous, paperback $8.95 (#51034)

How to Disappear Completely and Never Be Found by Doug Richmond, paperback $7.95 (#51559)

Prices subject to change;
books subject to availability

How to Get All the Credit You Want (and Erase Your Bad Credit Record) by Bob Hammond, paperback $6.95 (#51397)

Make 'em Pay by George Hayduke, paperback $8.95 (#40421)

Make My Day by George Hayduke, paperback $8.95 (#40464)

Mayhem by George Hayduke, paperback $7.95 (#40565)

Researching Public Records: How to Get Anything on Anybody by Vincent Parco, paperback $8.95 (#51522)

Revenge by George Hayduke, oversized paperback $14.95 (#40353)

Revenge Tactics From the Master of Mayhem: Hardcore Hayduke by George Hayduke, paperback $8.95 (#40575)

Righteous Revenge by George Hayduke, paperback $8.95 (#40569)

Secrets of Making and Breaking Codes by Hamilton Nickels, paperback $6.95 (#51563)

Undercover Operations: A Manual for the Private Investigator by Kingdon Peter Anderson, paperback $5.95 (#51166)